AFRICAN PATTERNS

Scrap Book Paper

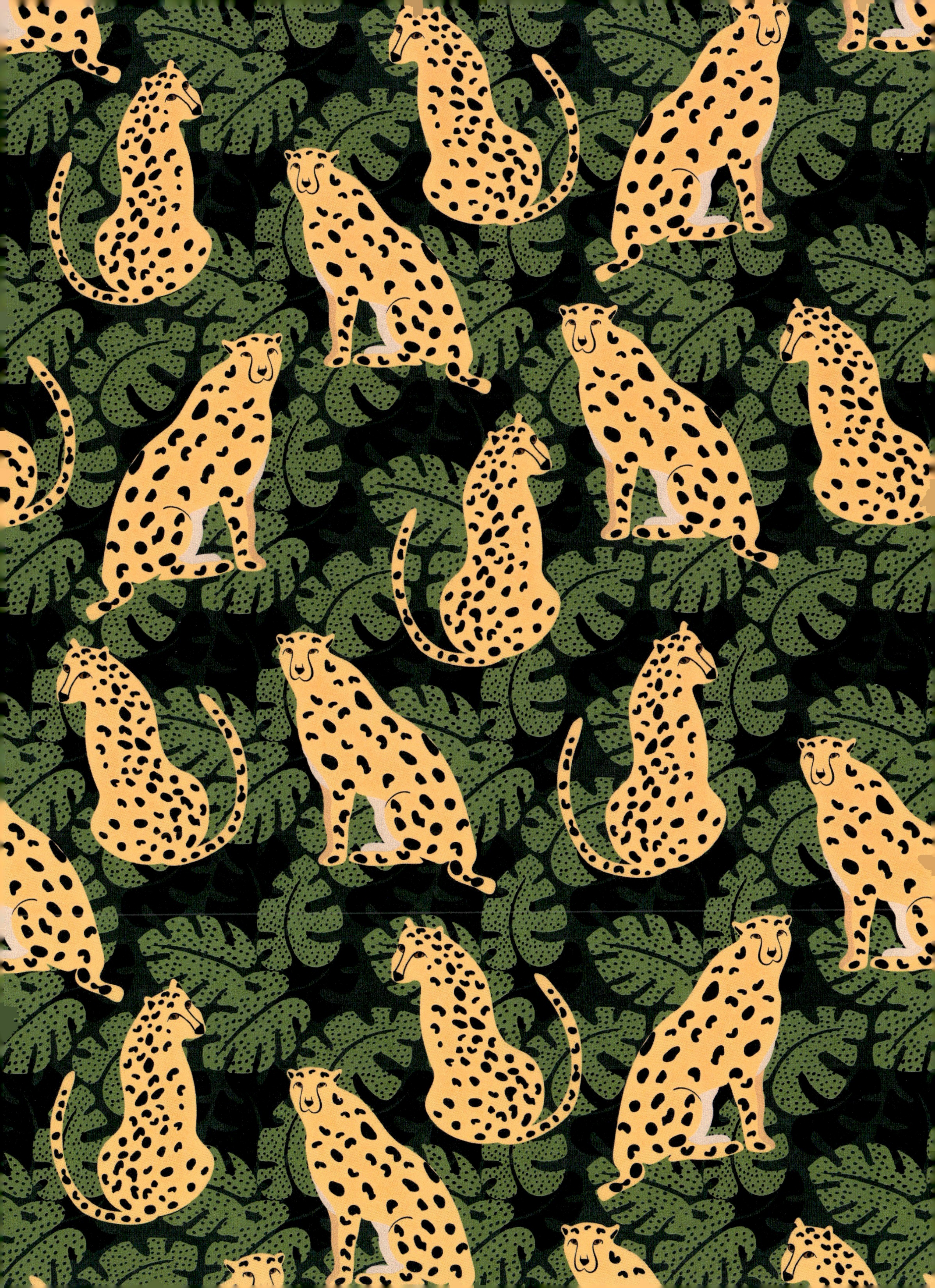

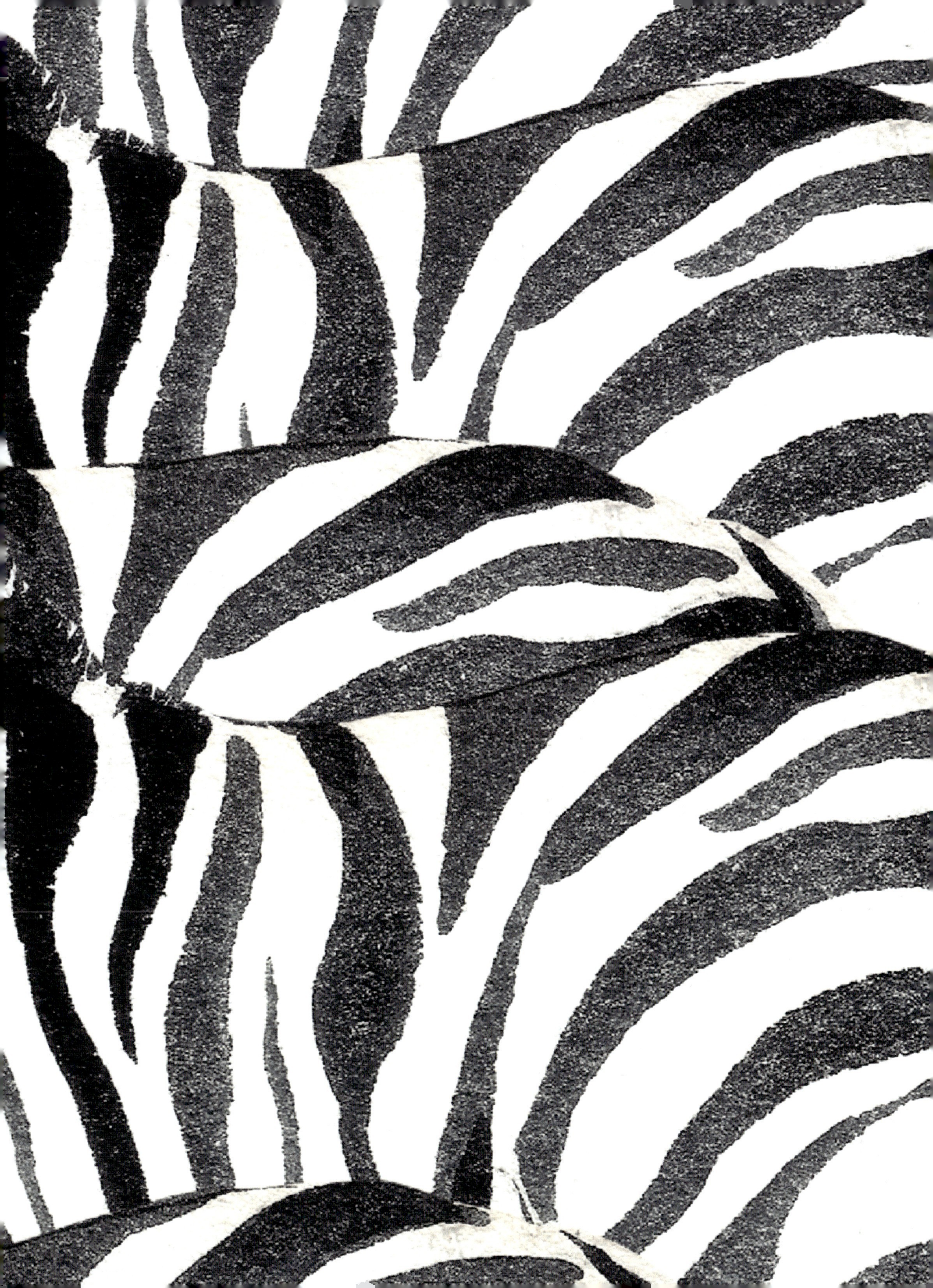

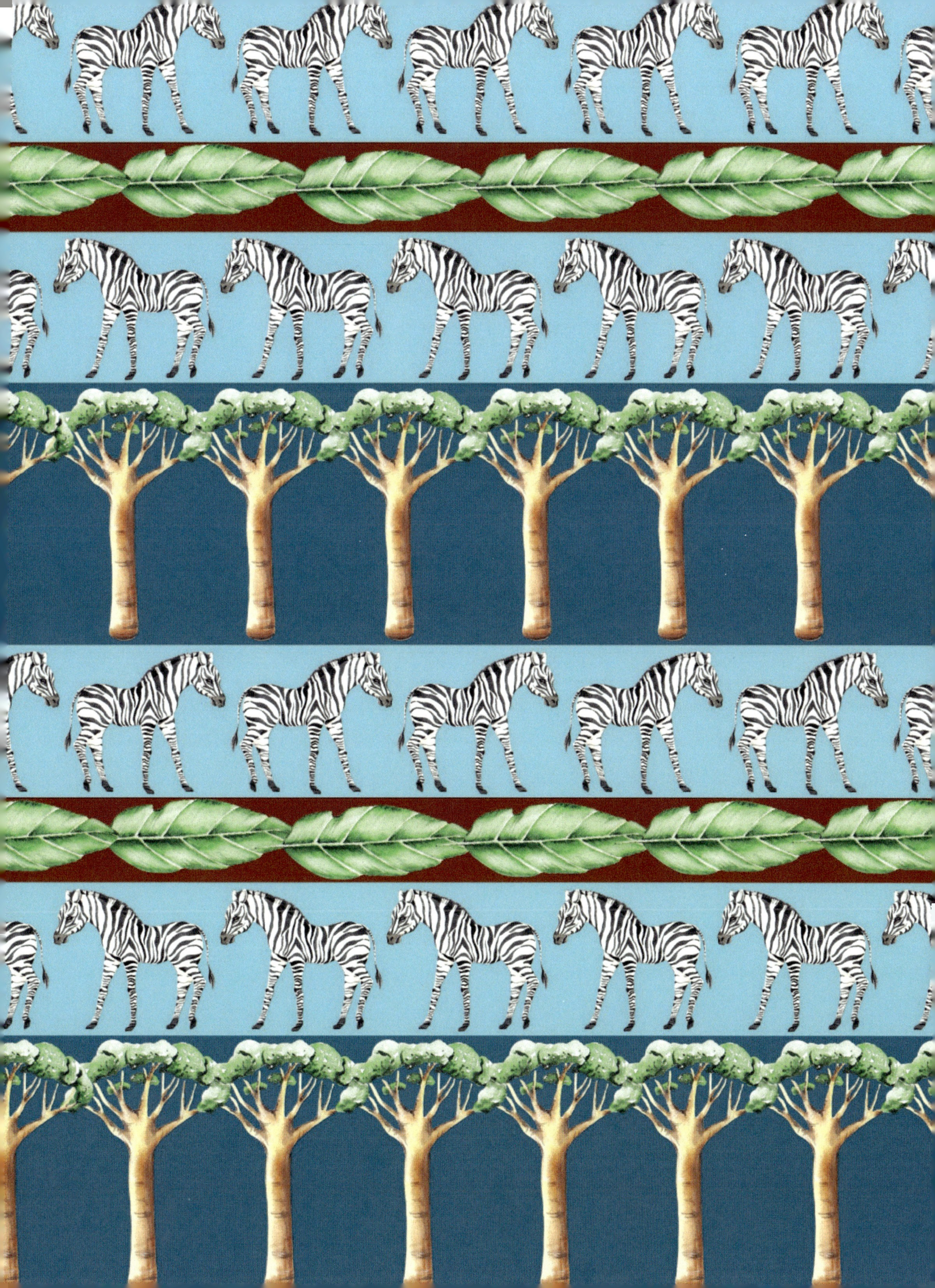

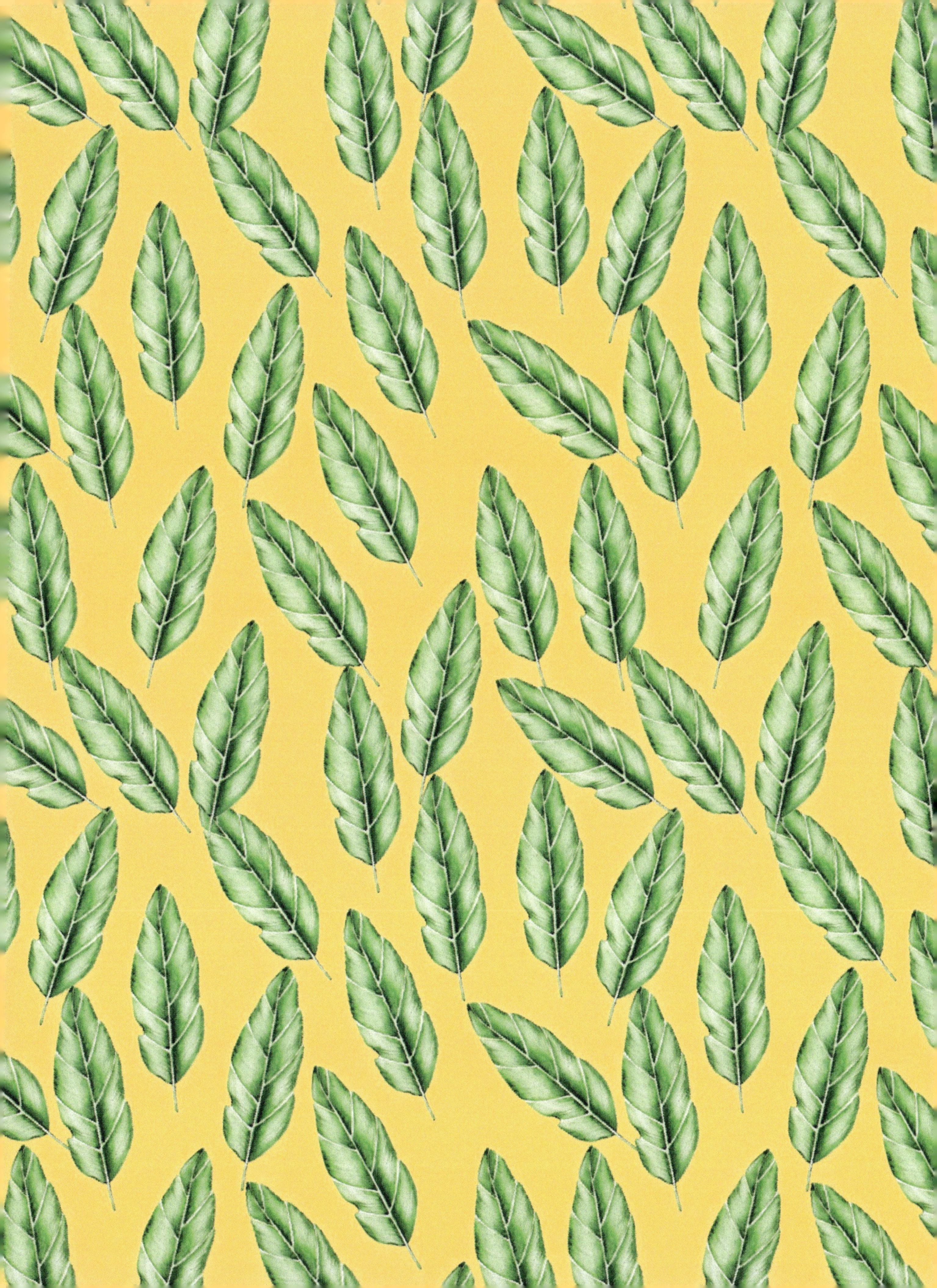

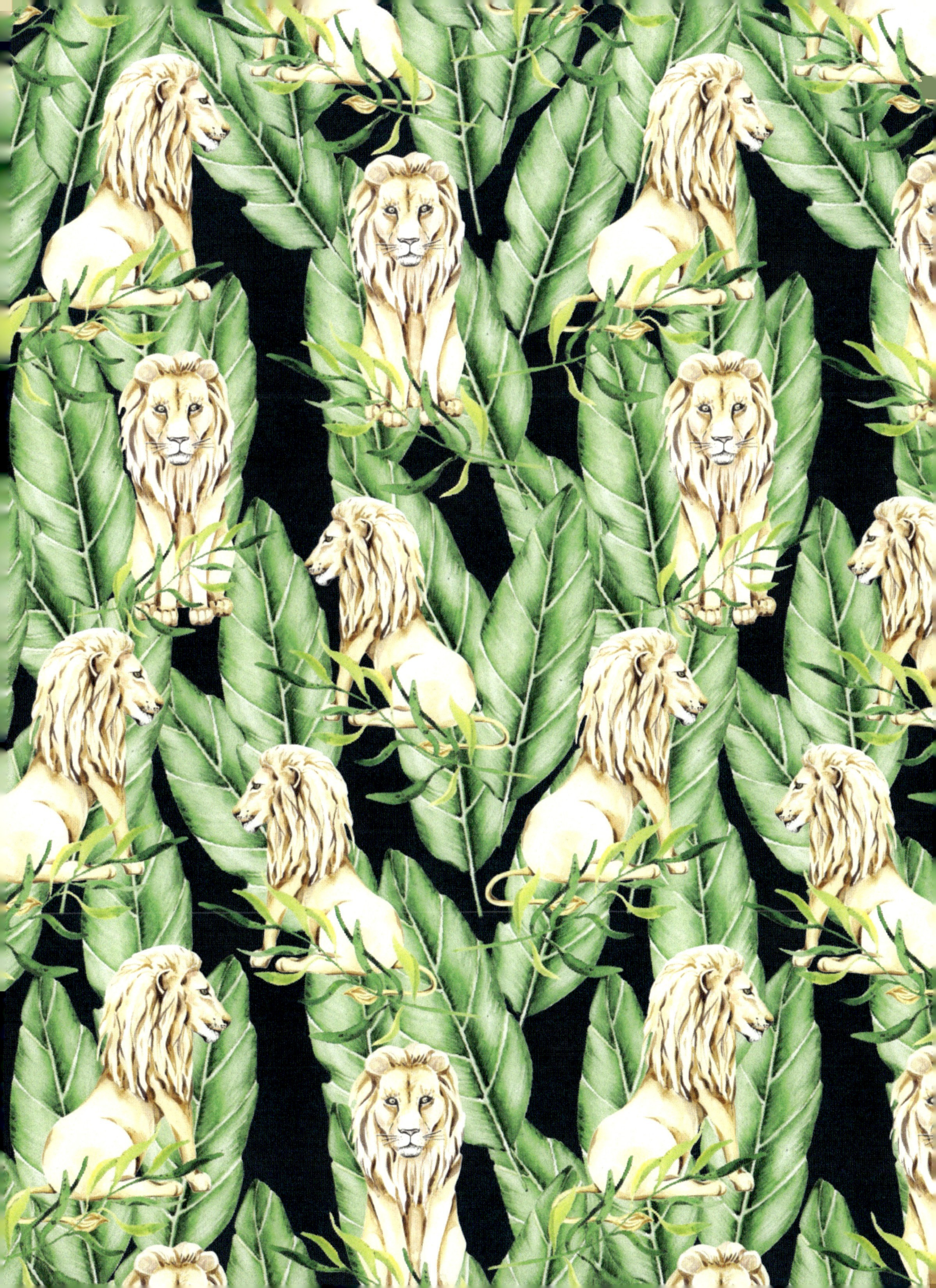

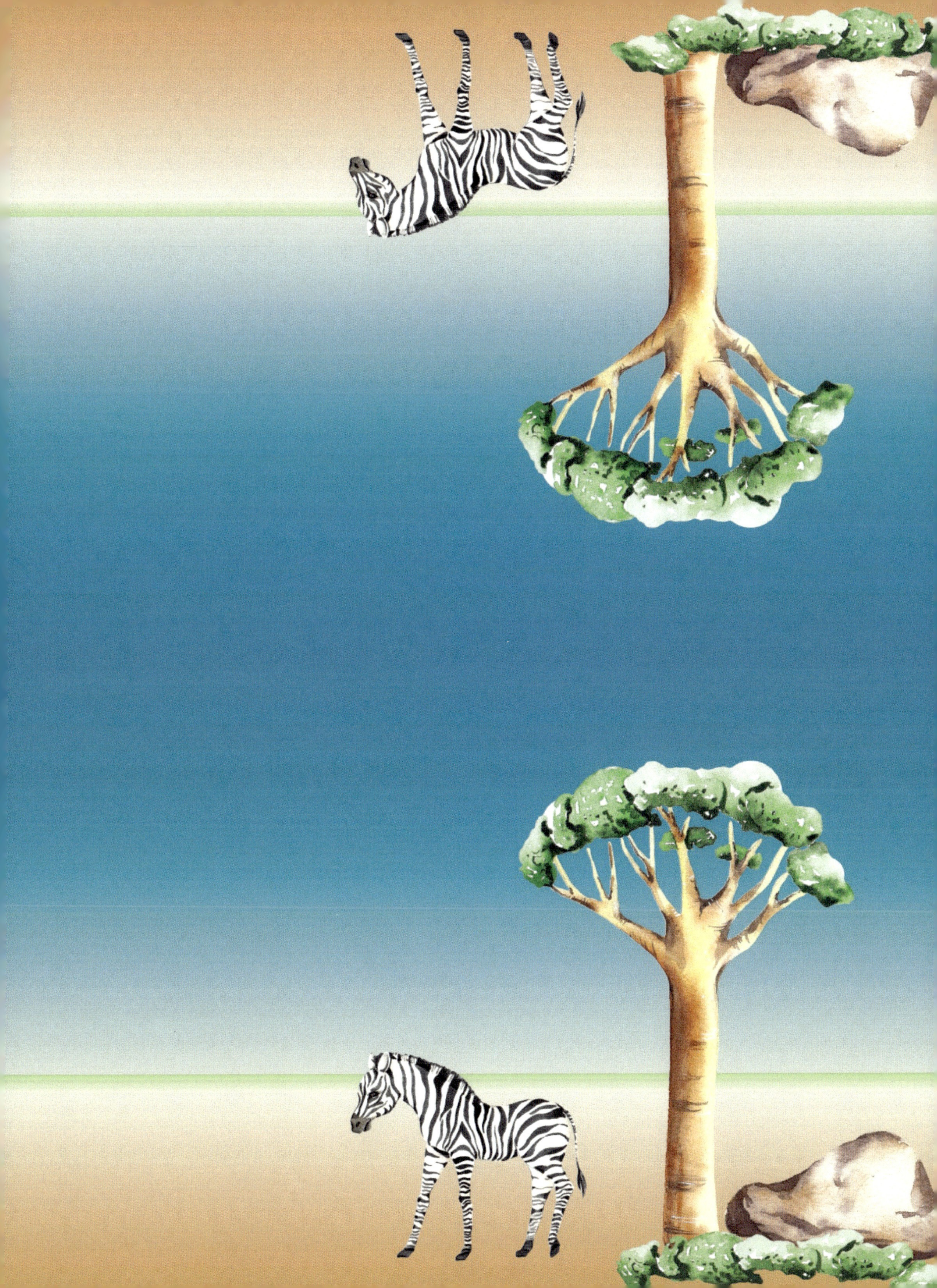

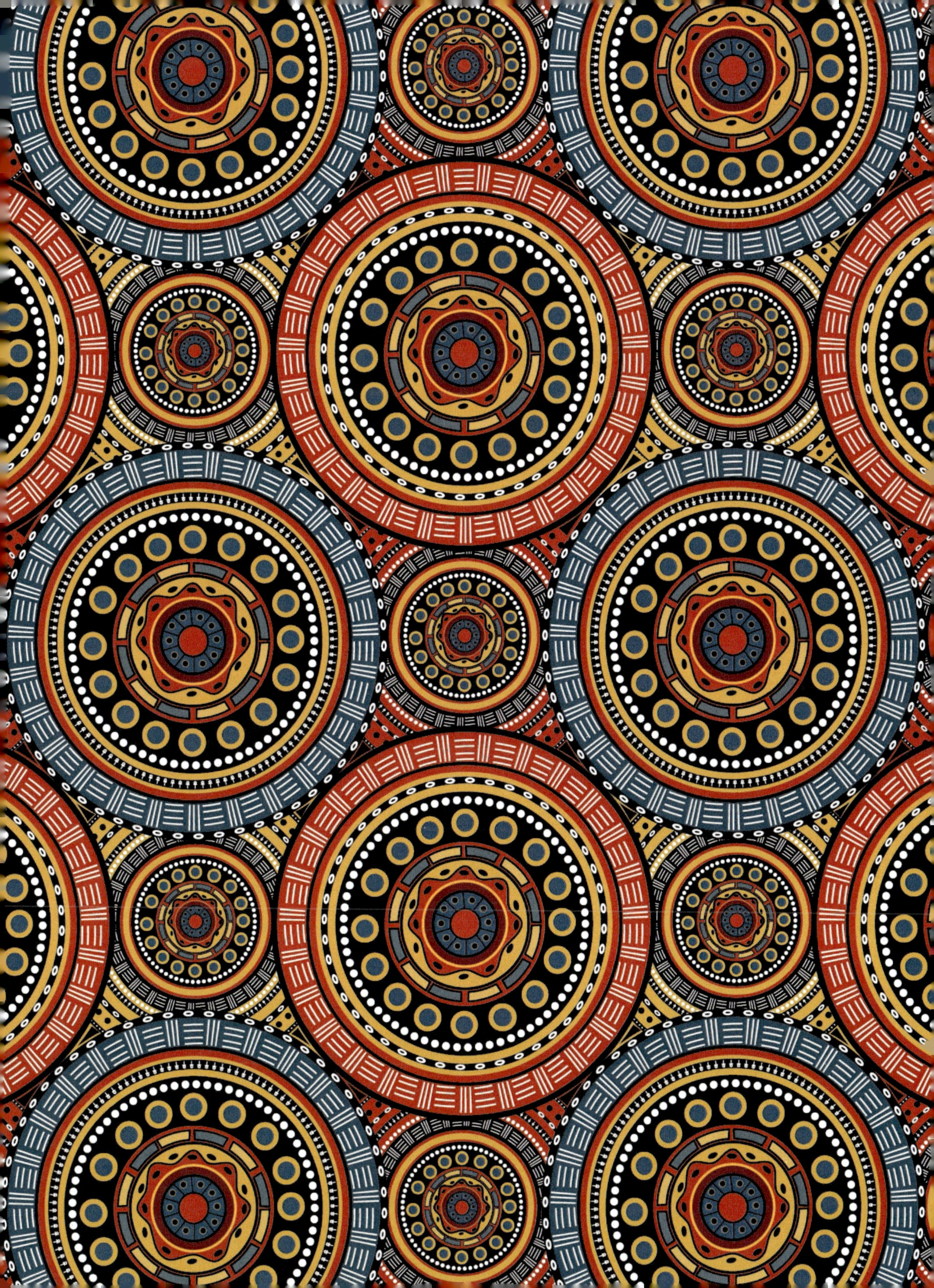

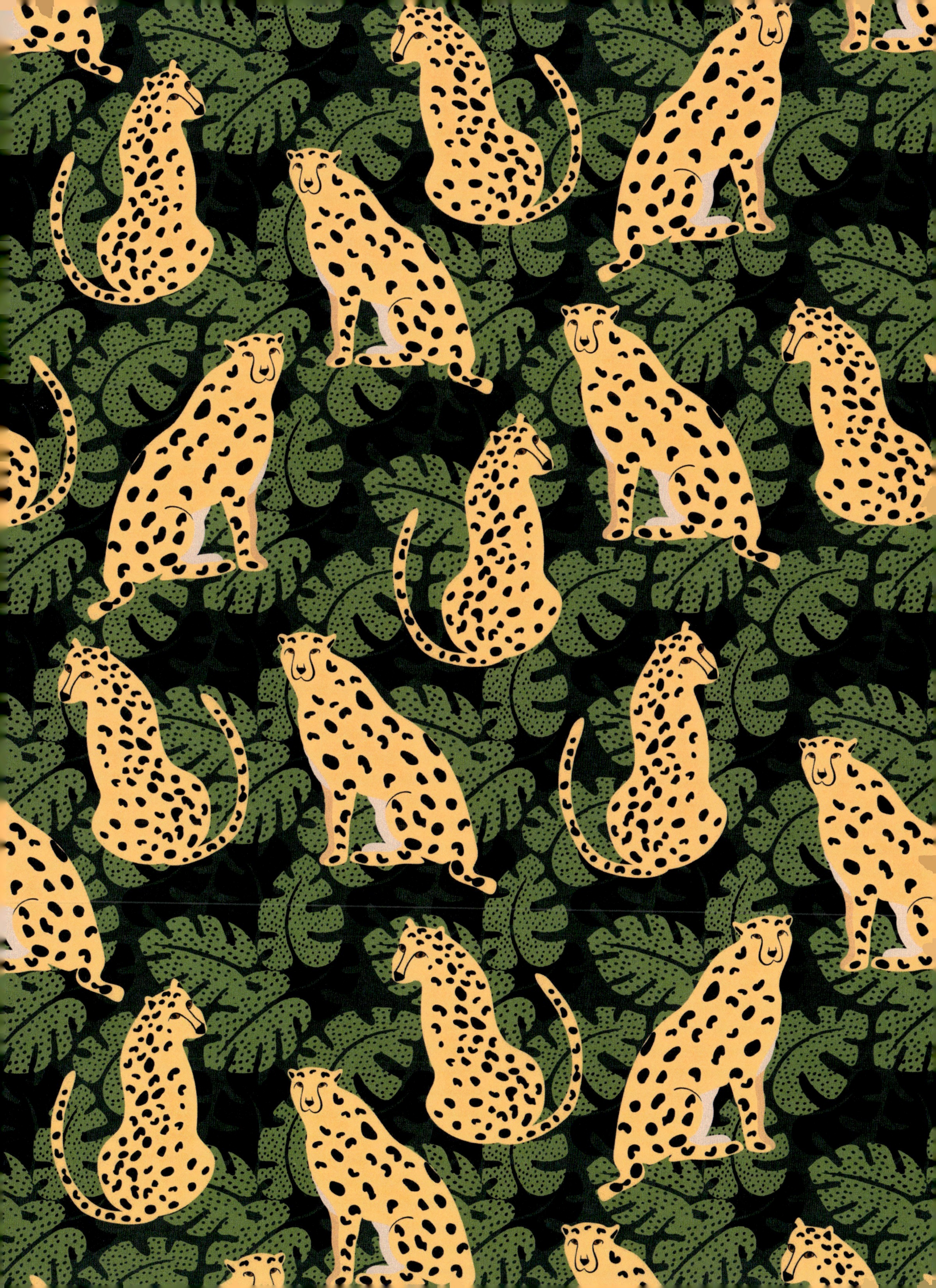

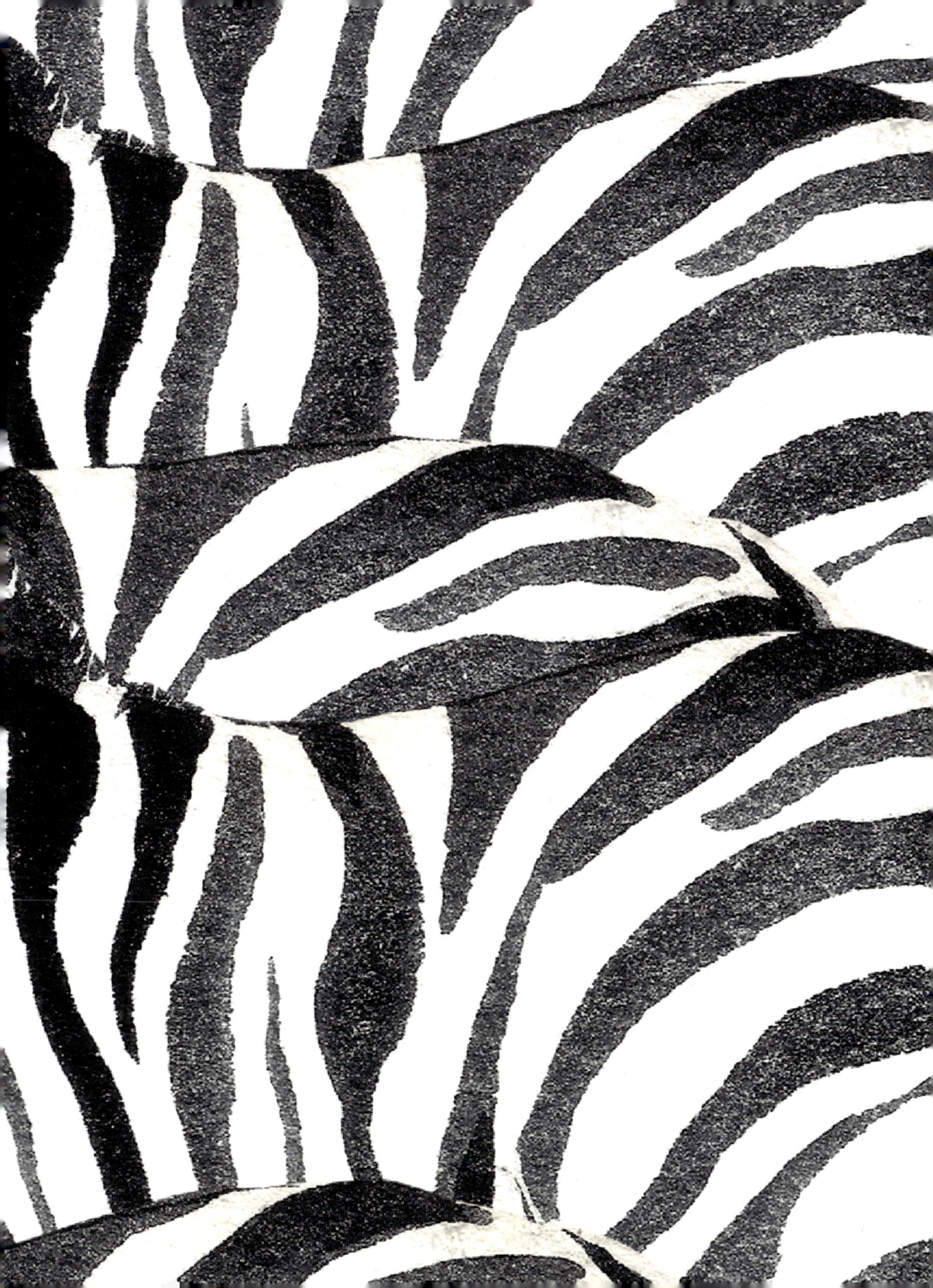

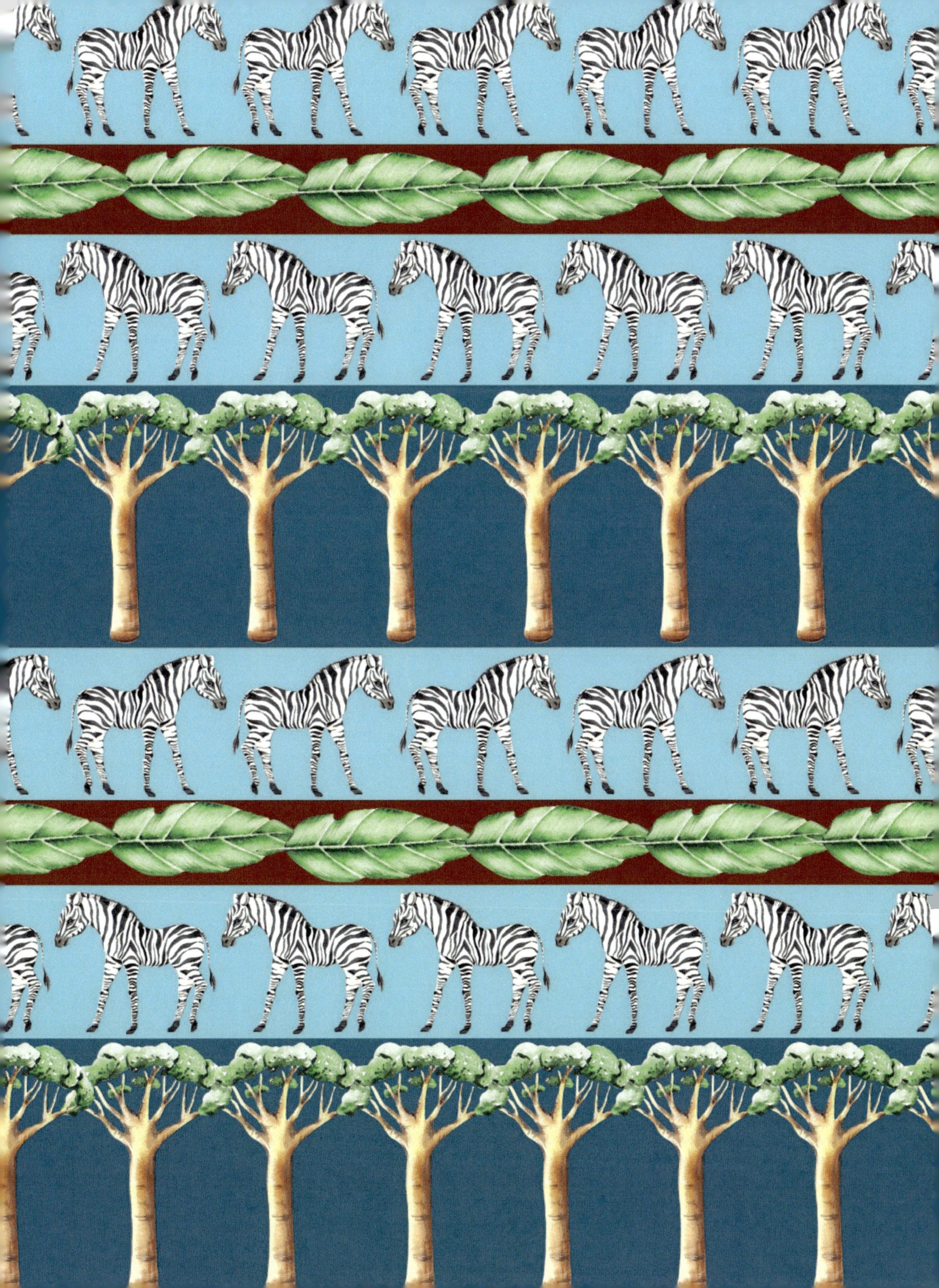

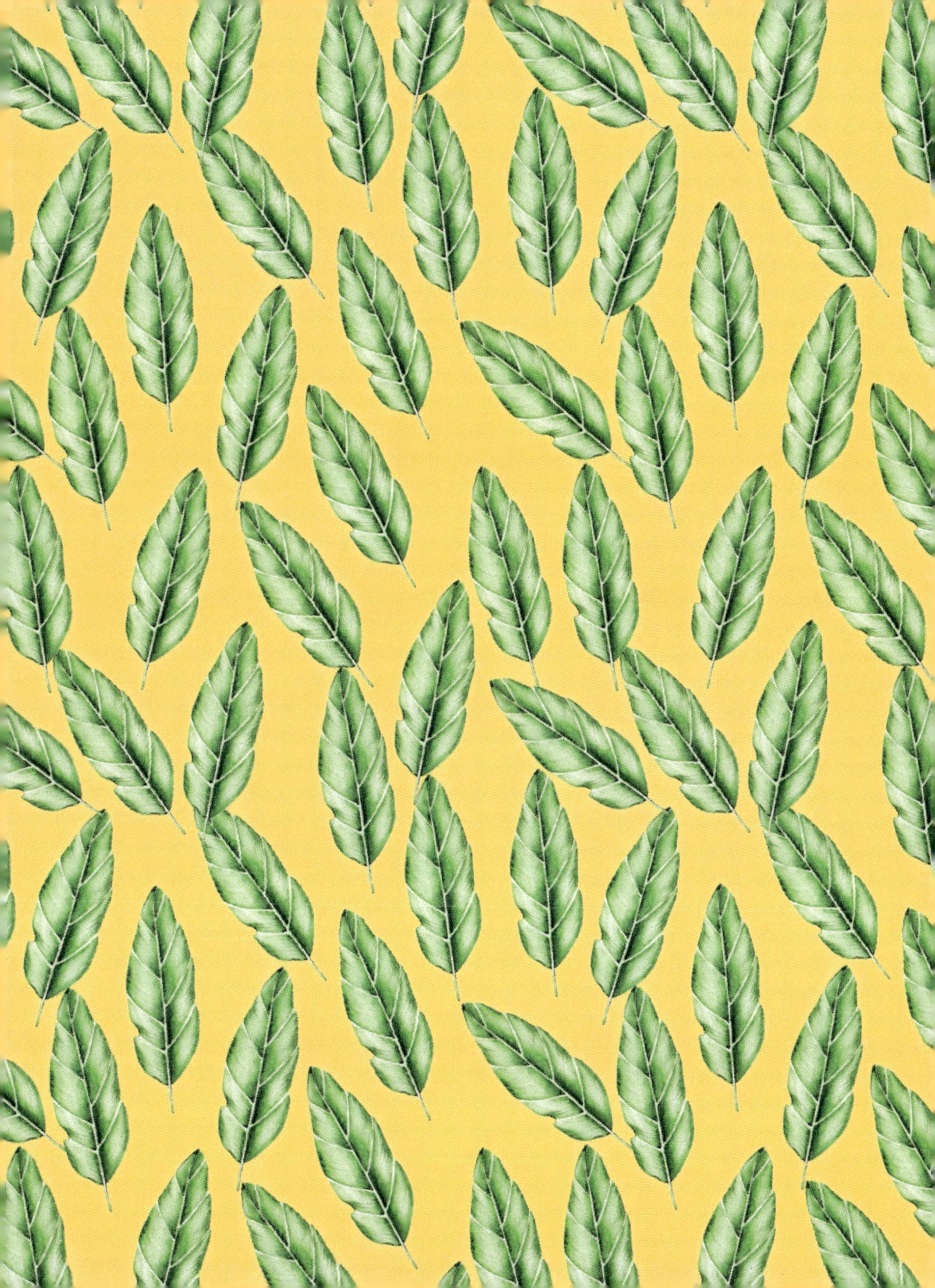

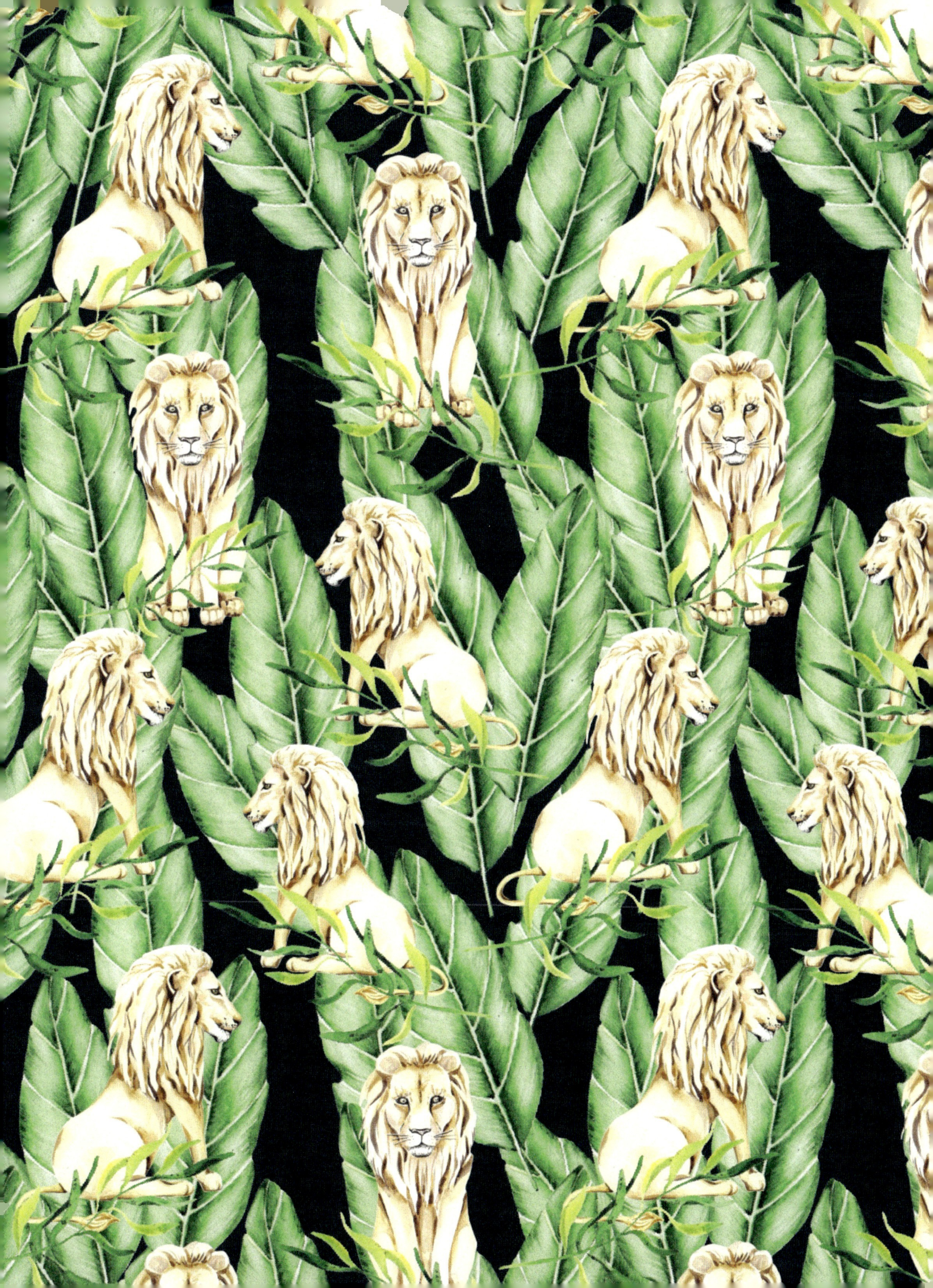

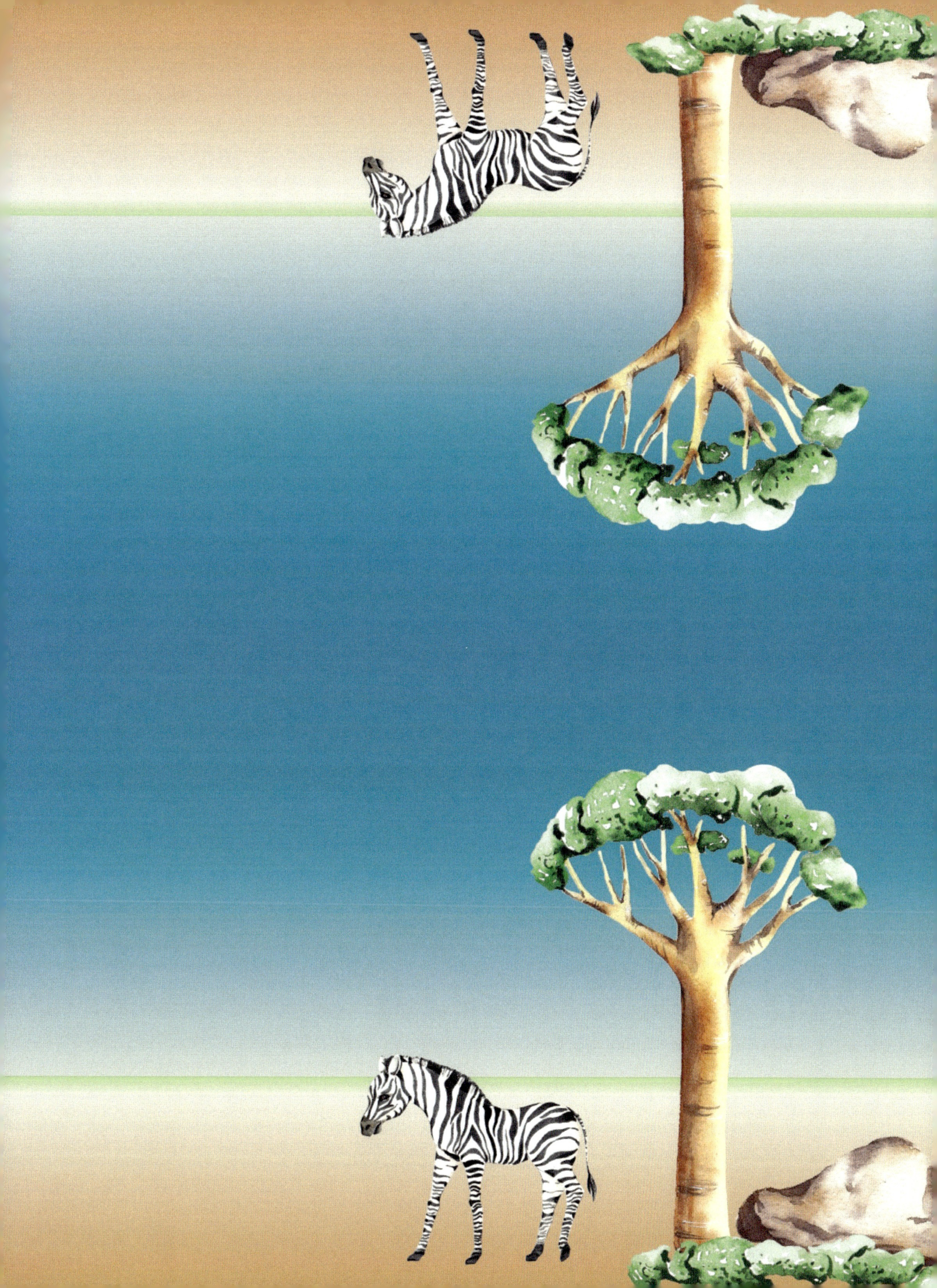

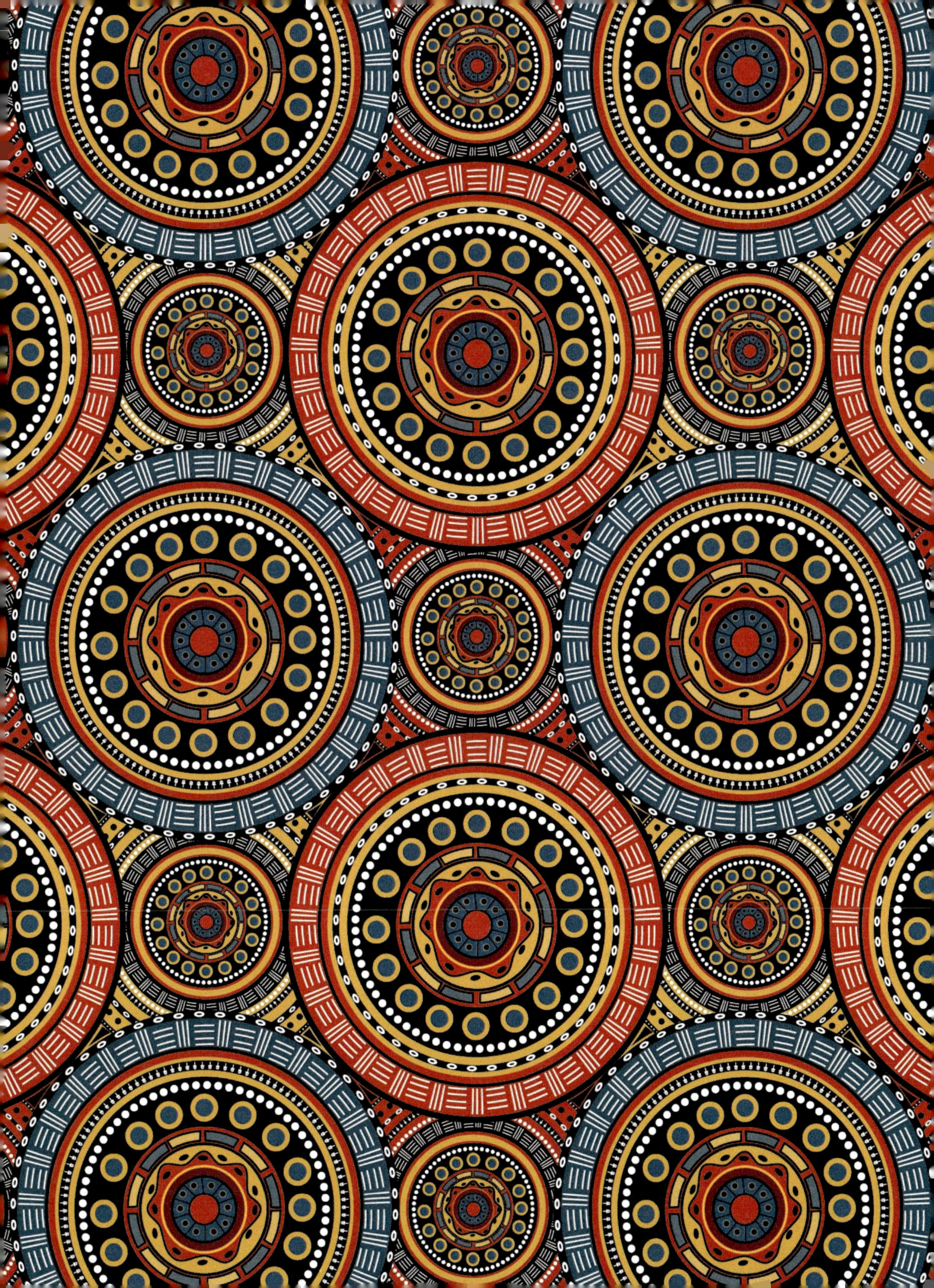

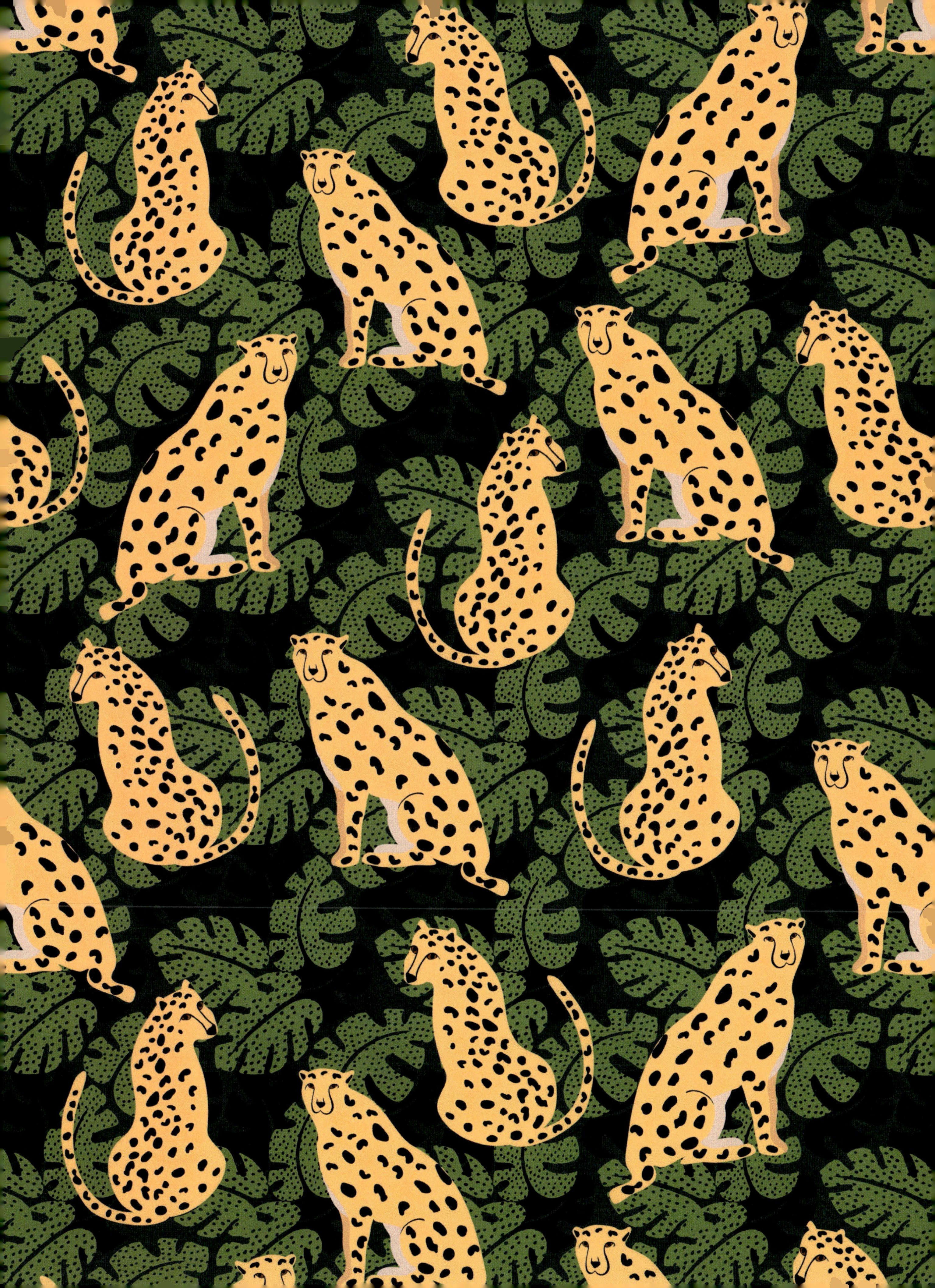

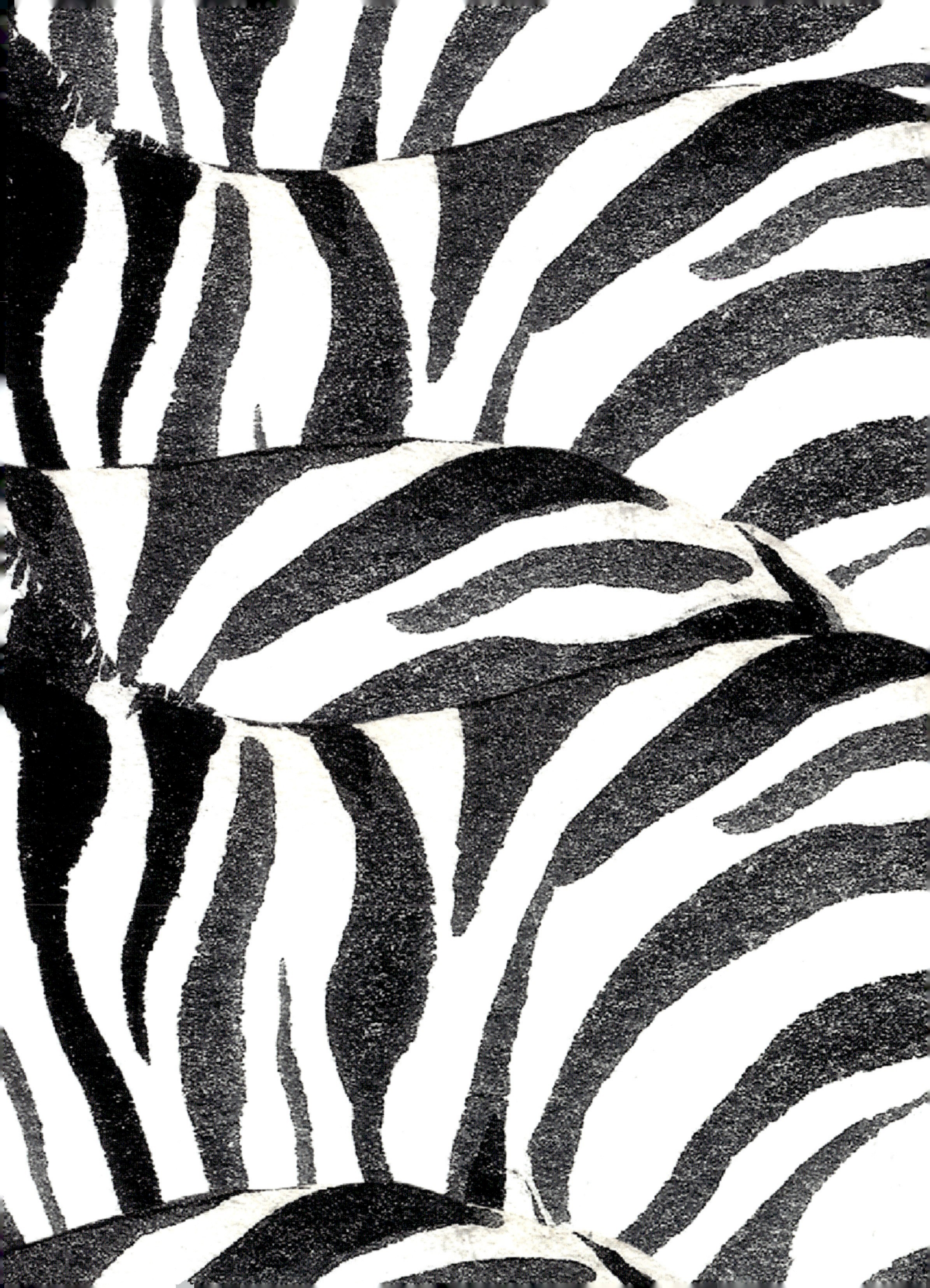

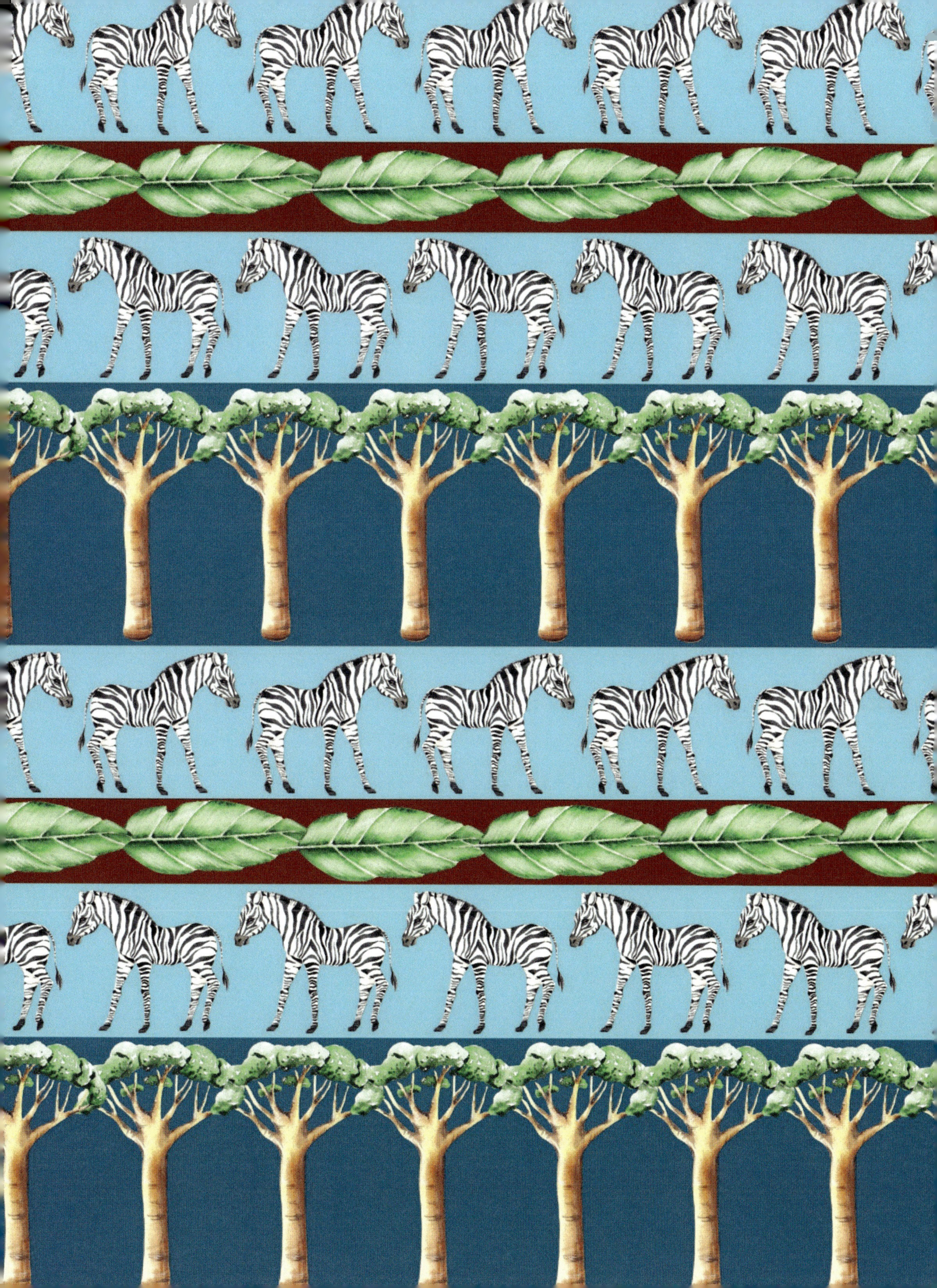

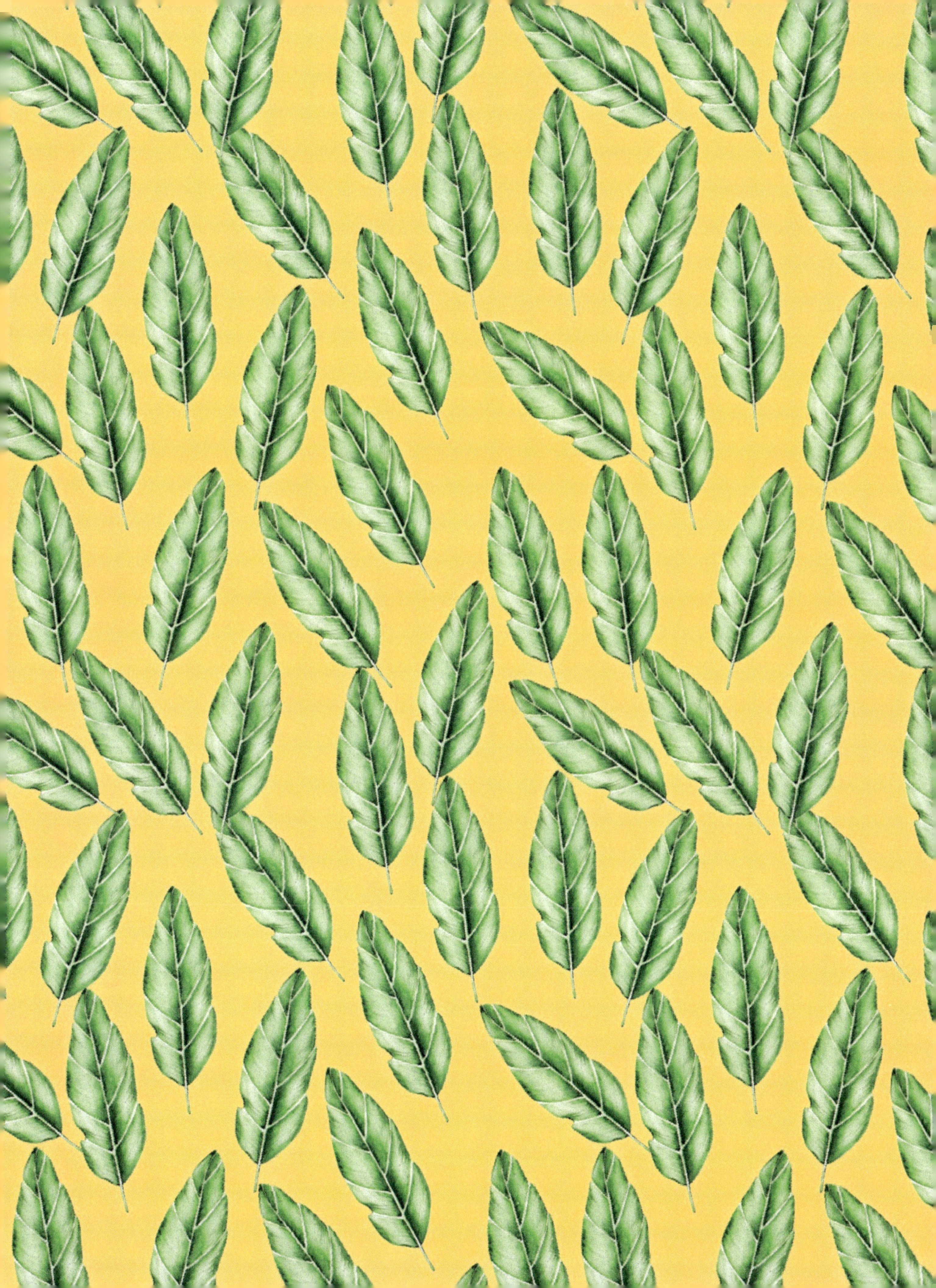

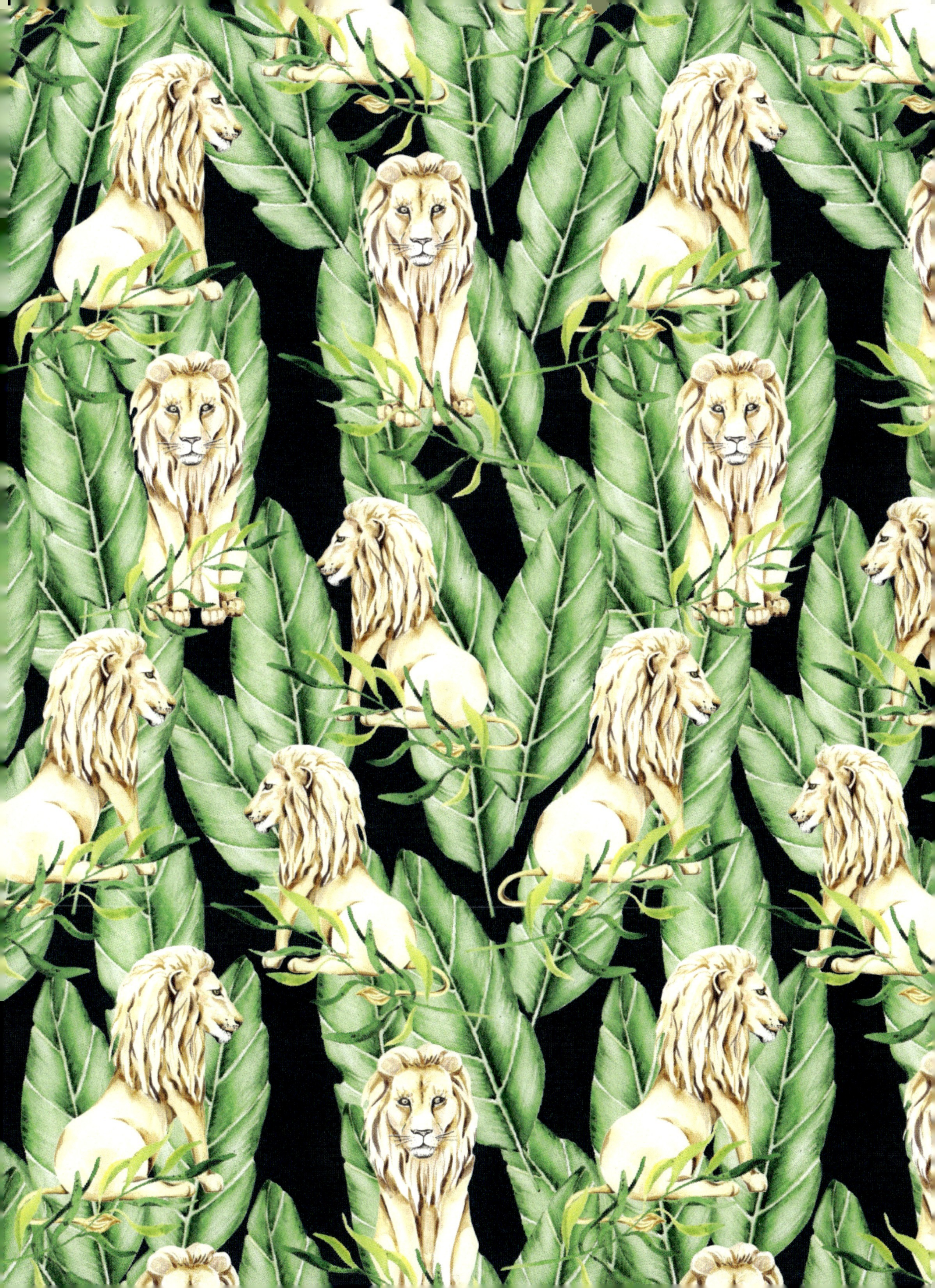

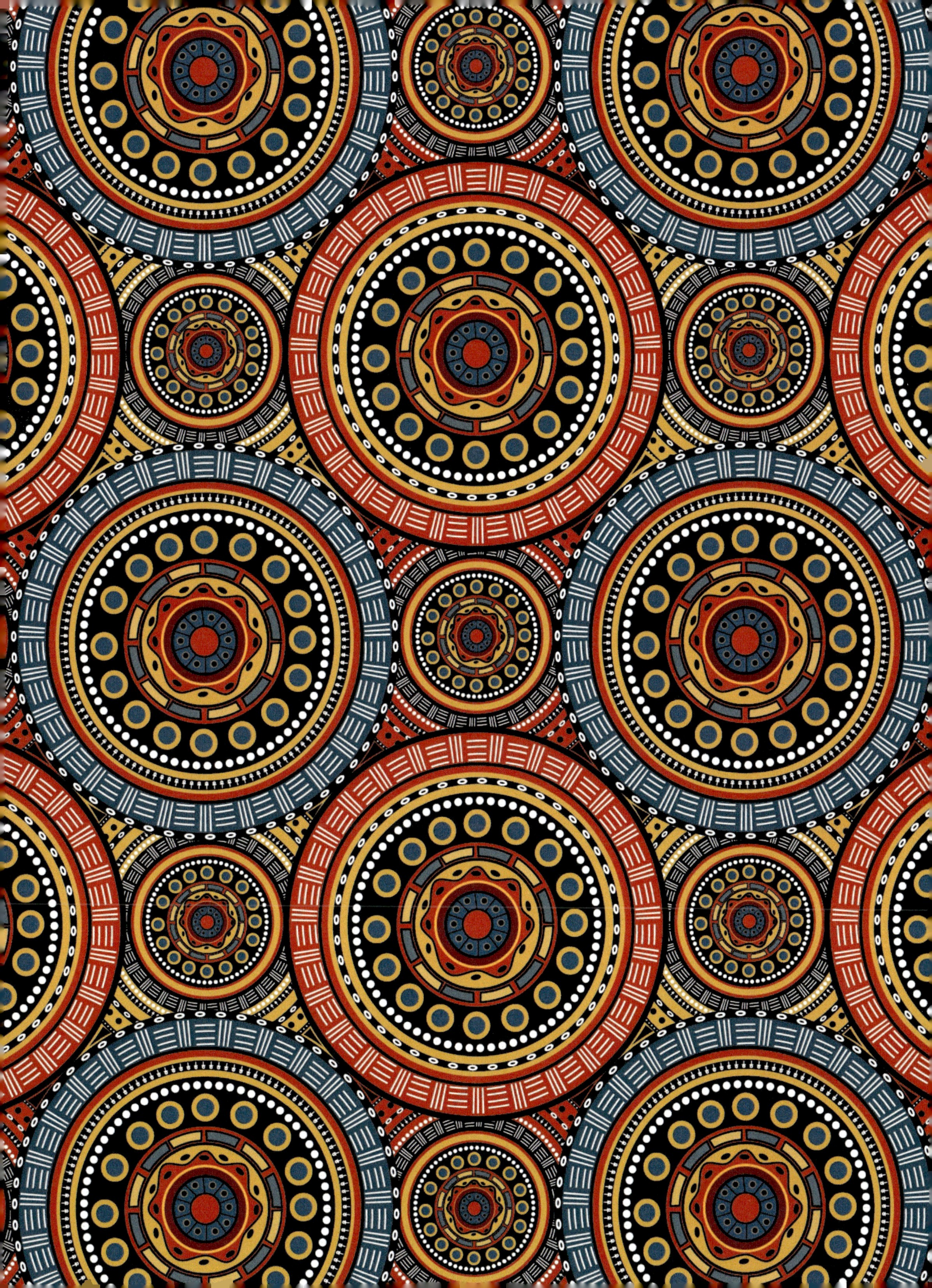

Made in United States
Orlando, FL
10 March 2022

15638693R00027